Relationship Resonance

Workbook

Bring Out The Best In Yourself And Others

ISBN-13: 978-1544651354

DEDICATION

This book is dedicated to all the people who have had a positive influence in my life. Thank you for all the wisdom, patience and love. I hope that the contents of these pages will resonate with the inspiration and happiness I have experienced internally and externally as a result and help to make the world a better place – one relationship at a time.

CONTENTS

Rationale   7

Encouragement   8

Quality Time   15

Understanding   20

Invest   24

Presence   28

Conclusion   31

References   33

RATIONALE

When people first encounter you, they quickly pick up on two things: one, your competence level, and two, whether you are helpful and friendly - or your warmth level. Moreover, they determine your warmth before they perceive your competence. So, simply put, people decide what they think of YOU before they decide what they think of your message at the beginning of every relationship.[i]

The good news is that, at any time in a relationship, you can achieve EXTRAORDINARY results by projecting both warmth and competence. You can actually elicit more positive behavior and emotions from yourself and those around you.[ii] This is the key to creating a wave of happy and productive people with you as the epicenter.

And these effects can resonate on and on and on . . . . The positive impact you make in another's life can create a new direction of influence as that person becomes a new origin that continues the effect. And it all starts with YOU. But don't worry. The Relationship Resonance system is designed to help increase your relational warmth and competence with our EQUIP model. This will help us all to do more and achieve more through relationship-driven success.

EQUIP is an acronym that stands for Encouragement, Quality Time, Understanding, Invest and Presence. When these components are active, my relationships flourish. When they are absent, my relationships struggle. And when they become inverted, my relationships decline. For example, using discouraging language in place of encouraging words.

Hopefully, the workbook format in the following pages will make it easy for you to understand and apply the system. Soon after filling out a few blanks with some heartfelt and sincere responses, you'll be on your way to making positive impacts on relationships of all types.

ENCOURAGEMENT

A little sincere encouragement could be the spark that converts someone's dying embers into a raging inferno. Encouragement can take the form of praise and compliments, appreciation and/or positive language.

Praise and Compliments

Make a positive impact today by telling someone what they are doing RIGHT. List the names of some people you know and a couple of things they do well. Then call, text, email or personally tell them. For example, Mary Ann is great at photography, so I'll send her a text message today telling her that.

1)_____
2)_____
3)_____
4)_____
5)_____
6)_____
7)_____
8)_____
9)_____
10)_____

TIP! You can make an even bigger impact with a compliment by elaborating on why you like the person's skill, how it makes you feel, or what effect it has. For example, I could say "Mary Ann, the pictures you take are so good that I want to hang them above the fireplace then pass them down for generations to come."

Add the feelings and impacts to the previous list and/or create additional ones.

1)_____
2)_____
3)_____
4)_____
5)_____
6)_____
7)_____
8)_____
9)_____
10)_____

Now do the same for yourself. Oh yeah, that's right! You have a lot of great qualities too. It's easy to let a discouraging environment keep you from remembering all the positive attributes you bring to the table. Jot down a few personal qualities, and frequently remind yourself about them.

1)_____
2)_____
3)_____
4)_____
5)_____
6)_____
7)_____
8)_____
9)_____
10)_____

Get some feedback from others on what they think you're good at or are doing well.

1)_____
2)_____
3)_____
4)_____
5)_____
6)_____
7)_____
8)_____
9)_____
10)_____

TIP! Feedback is crucial for helping us bridge the gap between how we perceive ourselves and how others perceive us. You may be surprised that people think you're great in areas where you feel that you struggle and vice versa. Moreover, the positive feedback can resonate for quite some time. So make it a priority to give and request feedback.

Appreciation

I'm sure you're familiar with the expression that it's better to give than to receive. Giving appreciation is no exception. Giving thanks and showing gratitude can actually improve the *giver's* emotional and physical well-being. [iii]

What are some things that you are grateful for?

1)_____
2)_____
3)_____
4)_____
5)_____
6)_____
7)_____
8)_____
9)_____
10)_____

Now list some qualities you appreciate in people you have relationships with. Then make an effort to tell these people what you are grateful for. As you did with your praise and compliments, you can make a bigger impact by letting them know how their qualities impact your life and feelings. A good old personalized thank you note can resonate for quite some time.

1)_____
2)_____
3)_____
4)_____
5)_____
6)_____
7)_____
8)_____
9)_____
10)_____

Revisit these appreciation lists frequently, and see how much better you actually start to feel. It is physically impossible to be both stressed and happy at the same time. Gratitude leads to happiness and, therefore, reduces stress.

Stress

Nothing discourages a healthy relationship faster than stress. Stress can definitely bring out the worst in all of us if we aren't mindful of its consequences. The good news is that most of our stress comes from our own perceptions and habits. We have the ability to reverse many stressful situations ourselves.

Name some things that seem to be stressful about your relationships.

1)_____
2)_____
3)_____
4)_____
5)_____
6)_____
7)_____
8)_____
9)_____
10)_____

Try applying these stress reduction techniques to them:

1) See the stressor as a challenge and not a threat. Try going into a situation with a character building goal, or see how many times you can count to ten before you allow a negative impact to affect your emotions.

2) View the stress as being predictable and controllable. Many of our negative relational outbursts stem from the following root causes:[iv]

   Controlling – Need to get a task done now

   Peacocking – Need for attention

   Perfectionism – Need to get a task done exactly right

   Overcommitting – Need to get along

   So knowing why we or others are behaving in one of these ways could lead to the ability to predict or control the situation.

3) Acceptance. Sometimes you simply have to accept the situation and try to make the next day better than this one. Worrying or ruminating only reduces your emotional and physical well-being.[v]

Doug Hacking

Now list some ways in which you can apply the above challenge, predict/control and acceptance techniques to your stressful relational situations.

1)_____
2)_____
3)_____
4)_____
5)_____
6)_____
7)_____
8)_____
9)_____
10)_____

Positive Language

The words we choose can either enhance or destroy a relationship in a matter of seconds. Learning to substitute negative words with positive language can lead to better relational outcomes. Even when we can't comply with a request or have to give some less than good news, positive language can improve the situation. For example, when a pharmacy customer presents an empty prescription bottle that is out of refills then asks me to fill it, if I say, "I *can't* fill this . . ." the interaction goes south. So instead I say, "OK. It looks like we need to call the doctor first to get you more refills. I *can* fill this as soon as we hear back."

What are some things that you have told yourself, or people have told you that you can't do? You can't run a 5k? You can't get a promotion because you're not qualified?

1)_____
2)_____
3)_____
4)_____
5)_____
6)_____
7)_____
8)_____
9)_____
10)_____

Now change the previous responses to statements regarding what you can do: I can run 1/2 mile today and then build up to a 5k distance eventually. I can learn what I need to achieve to qualify for that promotion then apply for it down the road.

1)_____
2)_____
3)_____
4)_____
5)_____
6)_____
7)_____
8)_____
9)_____
10)_____

What are some things you believe others can't do or have told them they can't do?

1)_____
2)_____
3)_____
4)_____
5)_____
6)_____
7)_____
8)_____
9)_____
10)_____

Now, using positive language, give scenarios that describe how they can do them.

1)_____
2)_____
3)_____
4)_____
5)_____
6)_____
7)_____
8)_____
9)_____
10)_____

Continually keep tabs on negative words like "can't," "don't," "won't," and "no." Try to keep them from negatively affecting you or a relationship. Then make an effort to step up your use of words like "can," "will," "do," and "yes."

One of the most positive words a person can hear is "love." Unfortunately, though, it's more common for us to let the world know what we hate. We hate this traffic or this place or this president. But "I love that" also presents a great opportunity to make a relational impact. See how you can do that? Next time you feel like saying that you hate something, vocalize your love for something else instead. For example, change "I hate all this traffic!" into "I love that I get some extra time with you in the car."

List some things you've caught yourself saying that you hate, and try to use a love statement instead.

1)_____
2)_____
3)_____
4)_____
5)_____
6)_____
7)_____
8)_____
9)_____
10)_____

Positive Body Language

Many times, your body actually says more than your content. Smiles, a straight open posture and open palms can instantly transform the mood of an individual, a group and yourself. In fact, smiling may actually make you live longer![vi]

Make a list of people to whom you will show off those pearly whites. Is it possible that some people you work with have never seen you smile? Then make an effort to smile around them.

1)_____
2)_____
3)_____
4)_____
5)_____
6)_____
7)_____
8)_____
9)_____
10)_____

TIP! A fake smile will come off as insincere, so try to think of things that make you happy to align the feelings with the actions.

QUALITY TIME

Setting things aside to make the people in front of you feel important creates quality time: moments of full, focused and uninterrupted attention. If you want to create the opposite situation with interruptions and partial attention, multitask the people around you. Multitasking can quickly wreck cars and relationships.

Multitasking

Activity:[vii] Use a timer, and see how long it takes you to write the following sentence and number sequence on the two lines provided:

Multitasking has consequences.

1 2 3 4 5 6 7 8 9 10 11 12 13 14 15 16 17 18 19 20 21 22 23 24 25 26 27

_____

_____

Time_____

Now repeat the procedure, but, this time, alternate writing the letters on the top line with writing the numbers on the bottom line (M on the top line then 1 on the bottom then u on the top and 2 on the bottom and so on).

_____

_____

Time_____

You should find that the second attempt took longer, probably had some errors, was of poorer overall quality and created some stress as you attempted it. These are just a few of the negative consequences of multitasking. The exercise represents what happens in our brains during the process because multitasking is really a misnomer. We are actually just switching quickly between different tasks.

The negative effects are magnified even more when we attempt to multitask in our relationships because, unlike tasks that can be switched on and off without regard, people have feelings and expectations. In fact, just having a cell phone out with the threat of potentially multitasking during a conversation can be enough to cause a conflict in a relationship.[viii] It can potentially activate the threat response.

Your time with others can be perceived as a threat or reward. So, to make your experiences feel rewarding, opt for quality time and utilize the following SCARF (Status, Certainty, Autonomy, Relatedness and Fairness)[ix] model.

SCARF – Status

A potential or real reduction in status can generate a strong threat response. Unwanted advice, lectures, pity and pride are just a few factors that can result in a status threat response. So, instead, keep the playing field level.

Pick some tasks that you would normally consider to be "beneath" you then perform them for the person responsible. For example, if you are the CEO of a company, take out the trash of all your officemates.

1)_____
2)_____
3)_____
4)_____
5)_____
6)_____
7)_____
8)_____
9)_____
10)_____

Now, pick some people in your life whose status you can elevate by giving them some of your responsibilities, time and/or attention.
1)_____
2)_____
3)_____
4)_____
5)_____
6)_____
7)_____
8)_____
9)_____
10)_____

TIP! Public praise and compliments can create a status reward.

SCARF – **Certainty**

We are all constantly trying to predict the future. Even a small amount of uncertainty can result in a threat response. So keep things explicit, defined and fulfilled.

What are some areas in your life that others may consider to be uncertain? For example, does your team know the dates and timelines of all the company's projects? Do people know when you're available? Do you have any unfulfilled commitments? Can people finish a conversation with you once it has started? List the uncertain areas then increase their certainty.

1)_____
2)_____
3)_____
4)_____
5)_____
6)_____
7)_____
8)_____
9)_____
10)_____

SCARF – **Autonomy**

The feeling of having no choices or input can result in a threat response. So surround yourself with the right people and let them do their thing.

What are some areas that you tend to micromanage? For example, do need to have other's items, tasks, projects or goals arranged exactly how you want them?

1)_____
2)_____
3)_____
4)_____
5)_____
6)_____
7)_____
8)_____
9)_____
10)_____

Now, give people a rewarding feeling in these areas with freedom of choice, creativity and flexibility.

SCARF – Relatedness

Not feeling like you're part of a group or clique can result in a threat response. So be sure to make everyone feels like they are part of the team.

Which member of the team has been getting the least attention? Do you have others around you who don't even feel like they are part of the group? Make a list of these people and, for each, give an action that you will take to help him or her feel involved and accepted.

1)_____
2)_____
3)_____
4)_____
5)_____
6)_____
7)_____
8)_____
9)_____
10)_____

SCARF - Fairness

Someone unlawfully goes before you at a four-way stop and you "go ballistic" because you had to wait for an extra three seconds. Why would waiting for such an insignificant amount of time upset you? It would upset you because unfair exchanges generate a strong threat response. So keep the scales balanced with equal transparency, communication and participation to your teammates.

Which group member may feel like he or she is getting less of your information, time and/or resources than others?

1)_____
2)_____
3)_____
4)_____
5)_____
6)_____
7)_____
8)_____
9)_____
10)_____

Quality Time – Uninterrupted Attention

Now, start sharing your full, focused and uninterrupted attention with others. Give a task your full attention and maintain it by eliminating distractions.

What are some of the things that tend to steal or shift your attention away from the person or task at hand? You can't list ten? Ask the people around you.

1)_____
2)_____
3)_____
4)_____
5)_____
6)_____
7)_____
8)_____
9)_____
10)_____

Try to keep these things out of your grasp (mentally and/or physically) to avoid the temptation of distraction.

Quality Time – Shared Focus

Completing an activity together to achieve a common goal is a strong quality-time booster. Even washing dishes shoulder-to-shoulder for five minutes can be big as long as both participants are in sync. This goes for planned and unplanned events.

Make a list of some people with shared goals or tasks you can complete together. How can you help carry the load?

1)_____
2)_____
3)_____
4)_____
5)_____
6)_____
7)_____
8)_____
9)_____
10)_____

UNDERSTANDING

Companies that show customers understanding enjoy a healthy return on their investment. The customers feel understood if their needs are met in an easy and enjoyable fashion.[x] The same goes for the people in your life. Are you easy and pleasant while meeting their needs? If so, I bet you're enjoying a nice return. Sometimes the need is for just a little bit of empathy. The key is to learn to remove our filtered lenses so that we can tie feelings and emotions to a situation.

What are some of the needs of the people in your life?

1)_____
2)_____
3)_____
4)_____
5)_____
6)_____
7)_____
8)_____
9)_____
10)_____

TIP! A great relationship builder involves simply asking, "What can I do to help you?"

Now meet the needs on the list above and remember to make the experience *easy* and *enjoyable*.

In good relationships, understanding is a two-way street. What are some of your needs, which you would like others to meet?

1)_____
2)_____
3)_____
4)_____
5)_____
6)_____
7)_____
8)_____
9)_____
10)_____

Take the guesswork out and kindly let others know about your needs.

Understanding Pathway

[See The Person/Situation] → [Listen] → [Process] →[Show Understanding]

Empathy is a tool we use to show others that we understand the feelings and emotions tied to their situations. It's a four-step process that starts with opening our hearts and ends with our connecting with their hearts as we show our understanding.

Step 1 – Eliminate Bias

If you want to halt all chances of showing any understanding to someone, begin the process by judging, labeling and/or categorizing them. However, if you want to make a positive impact, simply start by seeing the other as a real person who's dealing with a situation.

Think about and list how the following biases could possibly distort your perspective of a person's situation.

Anchoring Bias – Letting numbers influence and direct our thoughts
Framing Bias – Letting the way a situation is presented affect our decisions
Availability Heuristic Bias – Letting easily imagined and/or recent events outweigh past events
Confirmation Bias – Letting initial decisions become self-fulfilling prophecies
Commitment Escalation Bias – Not accepting sunk costs
Hindsight Bias – Once we know something, we can't remember when we didn't know it

Can you think of some examples where these biases may have negatively altered an interaction or relationship?

1)_____
2)_____
3)_____
4)_____
5)_____
6)_____
7)_____
8)_____
9)_____
10)_____

Try viewing the previous situations without the bias.

After eliminating the bias, try to see the other as a person with a situation and simply list that. For example, when my last meeting with my direct supervisor didn't go well, I could have let an availability heuristic bias keep me from remembering all the nice things he or she had done for me in the past. Then this bias would have negatively affected our next encounter as I would only have pulled up the negative encounter from my memory. So, to show my boss some appropriate understanding on my next visit, I need to first see him or her as [insert name], my boss, doing his or her job.

1)_____
2)_____
3)_____
4)_____
5)_____
6)_____
7)_____
8)_____
9)_____
10)_____

Step 2 – Communication

With the bias filters off, now it's time to open the lines of communication. So present yourself as someone who is eager and willing to listen. Then do exactly that – listen. Use whatever active listening techniques you have to pay attention, remain open and uncover the need that the other is attempting to explain.

The following is a list of the communication techniques you can use to uncover and verify details, feelings, emotions and situations. Practice them.

1) Be prepared to give people enough time to finish conversations.
2) Put your phone down and eliminate distractions.
3) Use open, inviting and positive body language.
4) Maintain appropriate eye contact.
5) Incorporate up-and-down head nods.
6) Use phrases like "Uh huh," "Tell me more," "Go on," "Give me the details."
7) Don't interrupt – wait for the speaker to pause before talking.
8) Pay attention to content, tone and body language (yours and theirs).
9) Paraphrase some of their dialog, Ex. "So you're going to Hawaii next week?"
10) Tie emotions to dialog, Ex. "I bet you feel excited about that!"

Step 3 – Process

Once you have all the facts, process the situation as if it were happening to you. This is where you put yourself into others' shoes. And if you have never experienced anything like their situation, try to imagine what it would be like.

TIP! If the situation is so extreme that it is impossible to imagine what it would be like, then don't try to act like you understand how they feel and accidentally simplify the situation. Sometimes a statement like, "I can't even imagine how devastating that would feel," has a better impact.

Think about recent situations that others around you have gone through and practice putting yourself in their shoes.

1)_____
2)_____
3)_____
4)_____
5)_____
6)_____
7)_____
8)_____
9)_____
10)_____

Step 4 – Show Your Understanding

Finally, demonstrate your understanding by repeating back what you have uncovered. For example, you might say something like, "Oh I bet you're excited to go on that dream vacation!" It's tempting to then judge their vacation choices or even start talking about your own vacations, but, instead, keep the spotlight on them.

TIP! Mirroring the emotions involved can increase their impact.

Identify opportunities to show understanding to the people around you. Instead of giving advice, solutions, simplifications or showing pity, get on the same level as the person expressing a need and let him or her know you understand the feelings and emotions tied to his or her situation.

1)_____
2)_____
3)_____
4)_____
5)_____
6)_____
7)_____
8)_____
9)_____
10)_____

INVEST

We all have an abundance of resources that we can invest in our relationships. We can give one or more combinations of our "5Ts" (time, talent, treasure, tongue, and/or tenacity)[xi] to the people around us.

But, before we invest in others, it's a good idea to make sure we have taken care of ourselves. That way, we can actually give our best. We need to put our oxygen masks on first as the airlines tell us.

Detox

Think about some bad influences, addictions or behaviors you can cut back on to become healthier, happier and more productive. We all probably have at least one unhealthy food, drink, activity, passivity, or thought pattern that is robbing our resources. Sometimes we can be unhealthy influences on the people around us and vice versa. Be honest and try to list as many as you can.

1)_____
2)_____
3)_____
4)_____
5)_____
6)_____
7)_____
8)_____
9)_____
10)_____

Now pick one, and try to eliminate it. It obviously won't be easy since willpower alone usually isn't enough. That's why the item is on this list. So find a healthy alternative to replace it and keep the unhealthy option out of sight, reach and mind.

TIP! Accountability partners increase success rates and can spark healthy relationships.

Diet and Exercise

We are what we eat. So I advocate spending extra money on organic and unprocessed foods to fuel yourself and on plenty of water. A healthy diet can relieve stress, enhance immune function and increase energy levels.

Make a list of some unhealthy diet choices you've made then provide a healthy alternative for each.

1)_____
2)_____
3)_____
4)_____
5)_____
6)_____
7)_____
8)_____
9)_____
10)_____

Thirty minutes of aerobic exercise daily are better than a commonly prescribed anti-depression medicine for improving one's mood.[xii] Walking counts as meditation and can reduce stress. Yoga can increase mindfulness, helping to make healthy decision-making easier. Moreover, a healthy physique increases your leadership edge as people are more willing to follow someone who models self-control and discipline.[xiii] So altogether, exercise can have positive benefits on your mind, body and relationships.

Make a list of some exercise activities you are incorporating or will incorporate into your weekly routine. Are you not currently on a program? Start slowly, but start something.

1)_____
2)_____
3)_____
4)_____
5)_____
6)_____
7)_____
8)_____
9)_____
10)_____

Rest

Sleep is a crucial part of any health program. Seven to nine hours of sleep a day will most likely meet the needs of about 99.9 percent of the people reading this workbook. Proper rest can also improve mind, body and relationships.

Incorporate some of these sleep tips into your routine.

1) No caffeine before bedtime: It takes three to seven hours for your body to get rid of half of the caffeine you ingest.

2) No alcohol immediately before bedtime: You eliminate one drink in about one hour. However, drinking alcohol immediately before bedtime interrupts your sleep pattern and prevents the deep-cycle sleep you need.

3) Keep from looking at screens or blue lights before sleep, and don't have remotes or phones within your reach.

4) Make sure the room is cool, dark and quiet. Use a sleep mask if necessary.

5) Exercise during the day. Running or workouts at least three hours before bedtime help your body prepare for sleep.

6) Avoid big meals before bedtime. A light protein snack is optimal. For example, eat peanut butter on a single piece of toast or a handful of nuts (not the whole can!) right before bedtime.

List some sleep strategies you will incorporate into or delete from your routine in order to improve your sleep.

1)_____
2)_____
3)_____
4)_____
5)_____
6)_____
7)_____
8)_____
9)_____
10)_____

TIP! A Fitbit can help motivate you and keep track of your diet, health and sleep.

Invest the 5 T's

Now you're ready to invest your time, talent, treasure, tongue, and tenacity in your relationships. It doesn't have to be much. Five minutes of attention, a quick demonstration, a fifty-cent treat, a two-sentence email of recognition, or a display of determination can have a lifelong resonating impact.

List how you will invest your resources (5Ts) in those around you.

1)_____
2)_____
3)_____
4)_____
5)_____
6)_____
7)_____
8)_____
9)_____
10)_____

Perhaps the greatest relational asset I've found to invest my 5Ts in where the people around me are concerned is capital F-U-N! Making a fun experience out of work, play and life has paid huge relational dividends. Herb Kelleher did it with Southwest Airlines[xiv], and I'm trying to keep his flame burning.

List some ways you can start incorporating fun into your work, home and social routines.

1)_____
2)_____
3)_____
4)_____
5)_____
6)_____
7)_____
8)_____
9)_____
10)_____

PRESENCE

We can keep people thriving with our presence. Showing up to events and being active can have a huge resonating impact on the relationships involved. It's as easy as 1, 2, 3 – get out, get active, make an impact.

Get out

If I suggested that you just start going to events that you normally don't attend, I doubt you would suddenly comply. So the first step is learning to get out of your comfort zone. Simple daily actions like brushing your teeth with the opposite hand or taking an alternative route to work can help get you out of your comfort zone as well as boost your brain power!

List some routines you can change up to learn to get out of your comfort zone.

1)_____
2)_____
3)_____
4)_____
5)_____
6)_____
7)_____
8)_____
9)_____
10)_____

It's difficult to project a strong presence when you're not physically present. So start showing up to the party.

List some meetings and/or events that you normally don't attend with your teammates. Then start attending them.

1)_____
2)_____
3)_____
4)_____
5)_____
6)_____
7)_____
8)_____
9)_____
10)_____

Get Active

Showing up is good for presence unless no one even knows you're there. So participate in meetings, initiate conversations and volunteer for projects.

List some areas that you can become more active in – then get active!

1)_____
2)_____
3)_____
4)_____
5)_____
6)_____
7)_____
8)_____
9)_____
10)_____

Physical Touch

The fastest way to make a connection is through the mother of all languages – touch. Touch can relay emotions and thoughts faster than speaking and can also result in the release of some feel-good hormones from the receiver.[xv]

High-fives, handshakes and fist bumps literally connect us and can constitute a powerful relational asset, so dish them out! List some people and the types of physical touch you will use with them.

1)_____
2)_____
3)_____
4)_____
5)_____
6)_____
7)_____
8)_____
9)_____
10)_____

TIP! Shaking hands with a subordinate can instantly increase his or her status and relatedness reward response.

Emotional Intelligence

Maintain a positive presence by keeping your negative emotions in check. Anxiety, worry, dread and anger can instantly wreck your presence. Counting to ten, taking deep breaths and changing perspective actually work well to keep negative behaviors in check.

Think about and list interactions that suddenly went south due to some negative emotions. Then list a technique from above, or one that you already have, that could have kept the situation positive. Practice staying positive!

1)_____
2)_____
3)_____
4)_____
5)_____
6)_____
7)_____
8)_____
9)_____
10)_____

Being aware of others' emotions is a big component of presence. Identifying a person in distress then reversing the polarity can result in a lifetime's worth of resonance. Others' sighing, crying, venting and sudden silence are signs that they are under stress. Making an effort to initiate a conversation with a "Hey, is everything ok?" lets people know you're *there* for them.

Initiate an open invitation to talk to some people you feel may be battling stressful situations. List the people and emotional cues you observed that prompted the conversation.

1)_____
2)_____
3)_____
4)_____
5)_____
6)_____
7)_____
8)_____
9)_____
10)_____

CONCLUSION

Congratulations! You made it through the Relationship Resonance EQUIP journey into your relationships. Keep it going, and revisit these pages as often as possible because, the more you EQUIP your relationships, the bigger the resonance field will become, leading to increased happiness and success. The results will include the potential for a huge positive impact on yourself, your relationships and the world. So I would like to wholeheartedly thank you for your time and effort.

Encourage – Be the spark that can convert someone's dying embers into a raging inferno with 1) Praise and Compliments, 2) Appreciation and 3) Positive Language.

Quality Time - Set things aside and make the people around you feel important by giving them your 1) Full, 2) Focused and 3) Uninterrupted Attention.

> Make your time rewarding with SCARF (Status, Certainty, Autonomy, Relatedness, Fairness).

Understanding – Remove the filtered lenses and tie people's feelings and emotions to their situations.

> [See The Person/Situation] → [Listen] → [Process] →[Show Understanding]

Invest – Utilize your abundance of resources to create healthy and positive outcomes.

Presence – Keep others thriving by 1) Getting Out, 2) Getting Active and 3) Making a Connection.

ABOUT THE AUTHOR

Doug Hacking received a doctor of pharmacy from the University of Oklahoma in 2000 and a master of business administration from the University of Central Oklahoma in 2005. He is a former pharmaceutical sales representative and works as a pharmacist, an adjunct member of faculty, and a relational consultant. He has over fifteen years of professional teaching experience and has devoted over twenty years to researching, practicing, and creating his Relationship Resonance system.

Dr. Hacking is a recent recipient of the University of Oklahoma's Outstanding Preceptor award and CVS Health's Paragon and Regional Preceptor awards. Doug resides with his wife and three children in Edmond, Oklahoma, where he attends and serves at Life.Church.

REFERENCES

i Neffinger, Amy J.C. CuddyMatthew KohutJohn. "Connect, Then Lead." Harvard Business Review. 02 Nov. 2014.

ii Fiske, S. T., A. J. Cuddy, and P. Glick. "Universal Dimensions of Social Cognition: Warmth and Competence." Trends in Cognitive Sciences. U.S. National Library of Medicine, Feb. 2007.

iii Robert A. Emmons and Anjali Mishra. "Why Gratitude Enhances Well-Being: What We Know, What We Need to Know."10 Aug. 2010. Web. 2 May 2017.

iv Brinkman, Rick, and Rick Kirschner. Dealing with People You Can't Stand: How to Bring out the Best in People at Their Worst. New York: McGraw-Hill, 2012. Print.

v Scheier, Michael F., and Charles S. Carver. "Effects of Optimism on Psychological and Physical Well-Being: Theoretical Overview and Empirical Update." Cognitive Therapy and Research 16.2 (1992): 201-28.

vi Munteanu, Monica. "Does Smiling Really Help You Live Longer?" Rivertea. 10 Dec. 2014.

vii Crenshaw, Dave. The Myth of Multitasking: How "Doing It All" Gets Nothing Done. San Francisco: Jossey-Bass, 2008. Print.

viii Andrew K. Przybylski, Netta Weinstein. "Can You Connect with Me Now? How the Presence of Mobile Communication Technology Influences Face-to-Face Conversation Quality." Journal of Social and Personal Relationships. 19 July 2012.

ix Rock, David. "SCARF: A Brain-Based Model for Collaborating with and Influencing Others." NeuroLeadership Journal (2001).

x Burns, Megan. "Customer Experience Index 2014." Measuring Customer Experience (2014): Forrester (2014).

xi Caine, Christine. In His House. Life.Church (2015).

xii Press, Ira Dreyfuss | Associated. "Exercise Found as Effective as Antidepressant Zoloft." Los Angeles Times. Los Angeles Times, 01 Oct. 2000.

xiii Dr. Carol Himelhoch. "Ties Between Fitness and Leadership by Dr. Carol Himelhoch." The Russells. 08 Nov. 2014.

xiv Freiberg, Kevin, and Jackie Freiberg. Nuts!: Southwest Airlines' Crazy Recipe for Business and Personal Success. New York: Broadway, 1998. Print.

xv Zur, O. and Nordmarken, N. (2017). To Touch or Not to Touch: Exploring the Myth of Prohibition on Touch in Psychotherapy and Counseling. Retrieved from http://www.zurinstitute.com/touchintherapy.html

Made in the USA
Lexington, KY
30 October 2019